Got Poetry?

an Off-Line Anthology
Second Edition (2006)

edited by
John Robert Powers II

A special thanks to Nate Hutnak, Tony Brown, Paul David Mena, Joe Fusco Junior, Victor Infante, Sou Macmillan, Ryk McIntyer, Deb Powers, Dave MacPhearson, Anne my wonderfully understanding wife, TJ, the Curators of Gotpoetry.com and everyone else who has helped to turn a website into a poetry community.

The publication of this book is made possible by the generosity of the readers and members of www.gotpoetry.com

©2006 Gotpoetry.com. All rights reserved. For information, address Gotpoetry.com 12 Strathcona rd, Cranston RI 02906.
ISBN: 978-0-6151-6534-9 (pbk)
1. American Poetry – 21st century. 2. Oral interpretation of poetry – Competitions. 3. Performing arts – Competitions. 4. Poetry – Competitions. 5
Poetry – Authorship. I. Powers II, John R, 1971- II. Title.

Contents

Retrospective	by John Powers	1
Girl Over Easy	by Deb Powers	4
The Dance	by Liv	7
Music: The Art of Hypnotic Recklessness	by Megan Andelman	8
Shhhhh	by Tony Brown	9
Because of You	by Susan Voth	11
A Soldier's Lament	by J. Bradley	12
The Beauty Inside	by Cody J. Czerniak	15
American Candy	by Ben Alan Brownlow	16
Show - Don't Tell	by Paul David Mena	18
EYES	by DIMITRIUS	20
The American Dream	by Mick Scott	22
Waiting on Maria	by Billy Burgos	24
Where Are The Voices?	by Afrika Midnight Asha Abney	26
Blind Man	by Bret Wooldridge	27
Step-Father of the Bride	by Joe Fusco Jr.	28
YO, HAMLET	by Ryk McIntyre	30
Series Letter #16	by Alveraz Ricardez	33
...Means Nothing	by Harris Shumway	35
Erotic Thoughts Of you	by Jenni Kalicharan	36
CAPE CANAVERAL PORNO	by Bruce Deitrick Price	37
Poem for Mazique	by Caitlin Meissner	38
The Geography of your History	by John Powers	40
Momma Said There Will Be Days Like This	by Kay Barcelon	41
You Are DOOMED!!!	by Victor D. Infante	42
Paper Dragons	by Mary Ward	45
If Only You Knew	by Melanie Reid	46
For Emily	by Jonathan Chin	47

Cabbages/	by K. Eltinaé	49
"The Neil Diamond Poem"	by Natey Hutnak	51
The Night Anna Got Religion	by CA Jackson	58
I Had Sex with My Mother-in-Law	by Randy Johnson	60
Bright White Polar Bears	by Michael Jeffreys	61
Haight Love	by Michael Firewalker	62
As They Retreated	by Zan	64
My Palestinian Girl	by Karim M. Sewilam	66

Since the printing press came into being, poetry has ceased to be the delight of the whole community of man; it has become the amusement and delight of the few.

-John Masefield (1878 - 1967)

GotPoetry.com – a retrospective

The past year has been quite a good one for GotPoetry. We published our first anthology, we debuted customizable poet pages, a finished poetry section, Page Slams, a new section for poets to list their books and CD's, and several new and great regular and exclusive featured columnists. We have also published over 2,100 articles and blurbs in the news section this year.

In March 2006 when we opened our Finished Poetry section, poets have submitted over 7,000 poems! The workshop forums are consistently busy with quality work.

In 2006 we served 6,674,644 pages compared to last year's 2,528,232 pages. That's over a 250% increase and means your poetic work is being read more than ever.

Our busiest month was December 2006 (763,838 Hits)
Busiest Day: November 7th 2006 (64,671 Hits)
Busiest Hour: 10:00 - 10:59 on November 7, 2006 (10,103 Hits)

On Wednesday, October 18, 2006 we had 761 Visitors on the site AT THE SAME MOMENT.

We added well over 1500 members in the past year and quite a few of them are quite active. Typically we have about 100 registered members a day swing by.

All in all we'd consider it quite a successful year.

For 2006 we will be focusing on refining the features of the site instead of increasing them. We have a good mix of offerings for poets and now we need to make everything just a little easier to use and find.
We will continue to focus on increasing content and poetic offerings especially ways to help poets hone their craft.

Please join me in thanking the great staff, contributing authors and curators of this site. Especially brownbwi, chameleon, hotstuff, jonathanchin, KenMoore, redheadedslxt, Sou, bardofaisle9, haikupoet, zork, scottwoods, ocvictor, rykmcintyre, Tony, and Natey. These are the people who help run this place. Without them this community would not be close to what it is today.

Most of all, thanks to the poets. Thousands of people, myself included, have really enjoyed sharing in your poetic work.

-John Powers

Head editor of GotPoetry.com

Girl Over Easy

by Deb Powers

The summer I was 19, I flipped
back and forth between being
hot child in the city and
mamma's fallen angel.
I was the kind of girl
who always found what she
was looking for. It was easy -
just walk through the door
of the nearest bar and
he'd be there, nursing a beer or
knockin' back a Jack straight up.

It was
easy. After all,
I didn't want much

a warm body, a hard
cock and just enough brains
to be out of my bed before
breakfast or sunrise, whichever
came first - as long as I came first

I was hard as nails
brittle as glass
and soft as the sigh
of a summer wind
that whispers yesterday
to lonely old men

and it was always easy
to be their soft touch
the wing on a prayer

the girl with the magic mouth
that left you inside out
stripped to the core
and begging for more

yeah, I was always easy
if you only wanted sex
the game of cat
and mouse or dog eat dog
was all the same to me, it was
all about who came out on top
and even when I wasn't, it was
always me.

He was 24, six feet tall,
blue-eyed blond with hair
that was my weakness - he
was different. He could have
stayed through breakfast into
dinner, spent the night and
started all over again.
We talked the day we met
for hours - passed a joint
and talked some more till
I was drowning in his words
as much as in his eyes,
imagining our fingers intertwined
and how my head would fit
the smooth curve where his
shoulder met his neck and I

knew how to play the game,
and did - fingertip to lip to draw his
eyes, a shift of shoulders
to let the shirt slide inch..by inch
every trick I knew to reel him in

and

when he leaned across the candle flame
to kiss me, the only thing I felt was
disappointment that they worked.

the dance

by Liv

Hearts pounding
playing silent music in their heads
nerves anticipating
every beat yet to be played
as if in a trance
skin meets skin
and they begin to dance
hands wrapped together
swaying in and out
of rhythmic waves
spinning all about
grasping her waist
he pulls her to him
molding them like clay
passion spilling over the brim
scents fill the air
as they become the dances slave
whirling about unreachable
taking all their wits to brave
losing all consciousness
but reason flees soon
they melt into each others arms
under the purple moon
souls entwined
they are blown away
by the sudden
harsh light of day
abandoning one another
the dance has ended
but soon fairies return to unravel
the dance will consume them, desire all but mended

Music: The Art of Hypnotic Recklessness

by Megan Andelman

Dim lights meet hazy smoke.
Eyes wander-
hands;
legs;
mouths.
Music echoes from wall to wall;
body to body,
the bass sensitizing the nerves.
Men throw down fifties and shotglasses
as women move rhythmically to the beat of the drums--
never having to speak; they let their hips do the talking.

A profoundly soused man embraces his new found confidence;
falling in sync with an exotic and mysterious woman
who smells of lavender and bourbon.
In the light her body glows.
Hands touch hands;
touch stomach;
touch breasts.
The music beats louder--
perfectly in tune with the progression of their pulses.
Blood rushes to and from each and every extremity,
causing the two strangers to introduce themselves
before smoking one more cigarette
and heading for the exit--
having spoken nothing more
than their names.

Shhhhh

by Tony Brown

who's asleep? everyone.
shhhhhhhh. don't wake
everyone up.

everyone's asleep. you can hear
mechanical things. power, water,
heat --

but bend closer (shhh) to hear
what awakens when everyone is asleep:

shades walking step-in-time
to all the breathing. shh -- you'll
see them, perhaps. they're thin

and pale, sometimes one is
grey or pink but most are sheer
and white.

they are commuting home
from their jobs -- moving the fulcrums
and tipping the levers that make
everyday things happen:
falling in love, screaming
at the boss, pool in a semi-dive bar,
test driving vans, counseling children,
daring to eat from a street vendor's stall.

they swirl away from everyone,
undulating, rising from the ground
once they've stepped past the sleeping
bodies, slipping through windows
and under doors.

you see that one hangs back.

she gestures to you.

who are you now
that she should want you --
are you another power like her
escaping from servitude? are you
a spy who's caught a glimpse
of something unheard of till now?

tomorrow morning
they'll all clock back in,
slip into their assigned bodies
and then everyone
will wake up and go back to work

except for you and her. you'll
stay with her and find out
where she belongs, her real name,
how this all started --

shhh. you have only so much time to work
on this. don't wake up. everyone
will want to know
if they see you've figured it out.

Because of You

by Susan Voth

he held her picture
across his chest
knuckles whitened
a look of pain
a fleeting moment
tossed into the fire
of shuddered nights
he held her close
and whispered a vow
to always love her
and promised eternity somehow
and silently
his beating heart stopped
and his last breath faltered
into the frozen moment
held forever there
he lay still
a soldier's death
upon the battlefield
a forgotten man
a praised trooper
an unwilling pawn
Mr. Bush
he lay dying
upon a foreign field
for you
Bush
because of you
He died because of you

a soldier's lament

by J. Bradley

let's get one thing straight,
we were never traitors
for we had no fists
to punctuate cries of revolutions.

we plucked weeds with our teeth,
dug deep underground to fill the coffers
of our princess's treasury
to keep the kingdom in prosperity.

and the thanks we got, keep plucking,
keep digging. my brother, Billy,
hasn't seen sunlight for months now
and his once proud chestnut hue
now a pale gray and his eyes, blacker
than the hatred filling me from the head
to toe.

if i had hands, i would clench them,
ball them into fists and beat them
against a chest i wish i had.

there are compromises one must make
for the greater good of a people
where outside perspectives believe
their choice as evil

but until you understand what it's like
to be a proletariat with lariats
cinching your people until their vitality
oozes out of them, you'll understand why
we chose the bastard child of a dragon

and a turtle
over a pretty pink princess
peeking out at her kingdom
from her throne.

we'd rather be foot soldiers for evil
than be treated as less than worthy
in a utopian society.

one regime's terrorist
is another regime's revolutionary.

i heard, before Princess Peach was taken,
she cast a final spell,
suckering two hapless plumbers
to save her kingdom from our new leader.

i have heard tales of their righteousness,
their innocent intent allowing our food and flora
to turn them into titans, burning fields
with their blazing sense of justice.

every day, the body count comes in.
my brother, Billy, now residue beneath
the one they call Mario's steel-toed boots.

if i could, i would cut his feet off
before delivering the final blow,
my own feet crushing his windpipe.

i know this is a war
we will eventually lose.

but i would rather die,
teeth chomping,
feet stomping,
charging at my enemy

with a soundless cry
than live in a society
that treats my people
as a lie.

The Beauty Inside

by Cody J. Czerniak

There is nothing more I see,
Than how she smiles and looks at me
It makes me feel unsteady
But she comes over to me
and I feel ready, to speak
Her thoughtful stare,
her beautiful hair
her eyes, her ears, her pretty face,
I notice nothing else in this place.
except....
The Beauty Inside,
that is where her brave, crystal tears are cried
I see into her when I look into her eyes, and am lost,
in the sea of thought
She always makes me feel better, when i am down
because she knows I will always be there, always in town
I'll be there in hurry, if she's hurt, in pain
because I know that she would always do the same
When I see her there is nothing else
Because I will always know that under that beautiful butterfly,
There will always be the Beauty Inside

American Candy

by Ben Alan Brownlow

America do you grow tired
of your wheatfield nightmares
and skyscraper blunders?
Do you grow tired of spent shells and ATM receipts,
barbed wire fences and caviar dreams
and the blood of ten thousand Mexicans
rolling over the banks of the rio grande a bayou of cherry jello?
America, just how fragile are you?
And what of your shaky monoliths,
cemented with child bones like the London Bridge,
Masonic cornerstone and tiny cogs,
creaking precariously against somber sundown
Like an obscene banner, like a quaking sword,
charging fiercely, the rapist's cock
Thud down the throat of the continent,
ejaculating trains and highways
straight through to uterus blue pacific ocean
conceiving the bomb
BAKOOOOM!!!
Uh oh, that was it! They dropped it. Reattach your sequins to
Your tattered tunics and dart your hand
Thru celestial fire for your handbag.
Does this genocide make me look sexy?
I understand we now have satellites astronauts TV dinners
and mutated grapefruits.
When do we cast our mutated grapefruits
at the iron figureheads, crimsoned with rust?
America, your forefathers are effigied in filthy green notes.
Candybars.
Imprisoned on your textbookpage.
America, I sigh.
You are a land of pet psychics. Aerosol cheese.

Glow in the dark Nikes. It took ten thousand fireflies
like dreams
to make the soles of your shoes.
In the land of milk, honey,
pet psychics, sex scandals,
we are all taking part in a livingroom dinner,
glass tit enshrined in the corner like a rediscovered masterpiece,
prodding remote controls like plastic nipples.
Warm sopor.
America, the rest of the world does not look to you for an answer.
They want you to ask the question.

Show - Don't Tell

from Got Haiku? by Paul David Mena

One maxim that is repeated over and over again in the haiku world is that one should never name an emotion, but should instead describe an action or an image that demonstrates that emotion. A few years ago I purchased a book entitled "May Sky: There is Always Tomorrow", compiled by Violet Kazue de Cristoforo. It is an anthology of haiku written in Japanese-American concentration camps during World War II.

It would have been perfectly understandable for the poets in this collection to dwell upon the shock, humiliation and despair of their experience. Instead, they used the medium of haiku to bring focus to their everyday lives, even if it involved being consigned to performing menial tasks:

many gourds hanging

on the darkened wall

cold wind

The words "darkened" and "cold" describe both observable events and lingering impressions without explicitly stating the latter.

rhododendron blooms

about to leave this house

where my son was born

In this haiku the author contrasts the blooming of flowers with the departure from home. At no point are we told that this is a forced eviction at the hands of a paranoid government, nor is that fact really relevant to convey the sadness of the moment.

winter night
sentry whistling
in the darkness

Here we sense the irony of a guard's whistled tune against the backdrop of a cold winter night. The writer's situation has left him without a song.

in the sage brush
two new earth mounds
torrid wind blows

Here the words "earth mounds" are uttered without judgment; that would be left to the hot summer wind.

There is much that can be learned from a study of ordinary haiku written during extraordinary circumstances. The simplest of language can imbue even the most complicated events with a depth of understanding that is the hallmark of a well-crafted haiku.

EYES

by DIMITRIUS

You were my confidence. You were my key, after all this time I couldn't see. I was blind, like a blind man feeling his way through a new house in the dark. Feeling his way around but never quite sure what he is really touching. I couldn't believe I lost you.

Lost you. Why and 4 what it doesn't matter. I lost you. It rings in my head. Why or why worry? This is how it has 2 be. I lost you. Yes. Yes. Indeed. DAM!

When I first saw you, I remember, I couldn't believe my eyes. You were like an angel
& a devil. Tempting me 4 more, But I had you by my side.

I don't feel the pain. I've been through it before. Let me tell you, Let me tell you, the pain, the pain gets easier 2 ignore.

Very rarely, do I ever rub my eyes

I feel no disgrace I still have my face. After all, "the pain is easy to ignore". They say that sometimes in life you must take a chance.

After all what is life without a little romance?

If your worried about the future then just "let go". We may not be here tomorrow to enjoy the show.

We can make money without having 2 sell our souls. Tell me how much you need and where you want 2 go.

They say go 2 church and try 2follow the bible.

But the roads the lord creates 4 us are only there 2 make us more humble.

So help me plant my seeds and let us try to live well.

Happiness is not always something you find on a shelve

Take it or leave it. But so with this I say good-bye, now that I have gotten the dust out of my eyes.

The American Dream

by Mick Scott

Is it me or am I just confused/
Someone has sparked this conversation and has ignited my fuse/
I'm mad at the thought of an American dream/
I say that I am mad at the thought of an American dream/
What the hell is an American dream/
I'll give you the answer and it's the American scheme/
What is set up for me in this U.S. of A/
Everything here is red, white, and blue, and the rest to me still seems all gray/
Can I get filthy rich from this American dream?/
Can I get a sip from the cup of this American dream/
With some of that American cream/
If you got one person that is rich/
We should we all get rich/
From the needle that stitched/
The American dream stitch/

I don't wanna hear about America being rich/
And wealthy beyond its cause/

If America was rich/
And wealthy beyond its cause/
We would have no homeless…wait a minute…let me pause/
And rewind back to the part where I said we would have no homeless/
Shall I press/
Unless/
No-one understood that part/
I'd gladly go back to the start/
For some of you that aren't/
That smart/

Doesn't anyone remember New Orleans in the wake of Hurricane Katrina/
And the aftermath that was left and the scandal with FEMA/
How many hours and days did those people have to wait/
Close to 16 hundred had to await/
Their fate/
An untimely demise/
Before someone realized/
At the last minute…Hey…umm…those people need help/
How should it of been spelled/
Out when you've got dead people swimming in kelp/

An American dream I have to laugh at that/
If you've got the American dream then pat/
Yourself on the back/
But if you work/
And you work/
And you still don't get paid/
And agree that the taxes are sky/
High/
And gas prices for your Ford Focus seems mathematical to an Escalade/
Then turn to your/
Neighbor/
And ask them with a scream/
WHAT IS THE AMERICAN DREAM///?

waiting on maria

by Billy Burgos

if it weren't for you
i wouldn't know
how to wait

squinting like some drunk
seeing brand new
daylight since
lastnights stupor

a chest filling with
the dioxides captured
on the teardrops
of lazy willows

if it weren't for waiting
at midday
i wouldn't know
what spills from
the underground

the scent of death
and age in a
cornered dustdevil
rising unexpectedly
heavenward

if not for maria
i wouldn't have the patience
to ponder gentle possibility

the hot pink sprouts
of thorny bushes

spilling over fences
office buildings meeting
backyards and embracing

i wouldn't know that
even with the sun
rippling distant streets

the wind filters cold air
through the upswept windows
or that my reflection
uglies in plexiglass storefronts

none of this i would know
if not for waiting
on maria to show

Where Are The Voices?

by Afrika Midnight Asha Abney

Where Are The Voices?
that echoes in the wilderness
beyond the seas and caves
stop abandoning
little brown boys and little brown girls

Where Are The Voices?
that stand in harmony
living the words and messages of our great leaders
Rev. Dr.Martin L.King, Jr.
and
Malcolm X

Where Are The Voices?
that strives for justice
for our people

Where Are The Voices?
that struggle to protect their
family

Where Are The Voices?

blind man

by Bret Wooldridge

blind man---
a photo of the wind
in his wallet

Step-father of the Bride
by Joe Fusco Jr.

I'm the step-father of the bride. I split the cost of the wedding with the father of the bride but negotiate all the arrangements because I'm the bigger prick.

My mantra is "half your money now, half right after the wedding, just in case you sucked!"

I'm the step-father of the bride. I look incredulously at the DJ who tells me it's $800 for the regular service and $1,000 for him to be interactive with the wedding guests.

"So for $800, we get a freakin' mime," I ask.
I'm the step-father of the bride. I look incredulously at the caterer who tells me it's a dollar for each piece of wedding cake they slice.

"How about if you just slice it in half and everyone just grabs a freakin' chunk," I suggest.

I don't mind being the prick of the wedding party. It's my nature to tell the Courtyard Marriot that the bride and groom will be in the honeymoon suite, one way or the other, despite the miscommunication on the reservations. I'm polite but resolute like a pit bull with manners.

I don't mind being the prick of the wedding party. It's my nature to tell MetroWest Limousine that their back-seat smells like cat-piss and their driver looks like Charlie Manson. I'm low-key but lethal like a napping cobra.

I'm the step-father of the bride. When my daughter and I dance to our song at the wedding and she thanks me for everything I've done, my "prickly" demeanor melts like warm butter on Italian toast.

"Anything for you, honey," I reply then bark at the photographer to make certain he captures the freakin' moment!

YO, HAMLET

by Ryk McIntyre

YO, HAMLET

Put your hands in the air and sing with me,
"To Be Or Not To Be!"
Wave your hands like this, if you don't wanna live!
"To Be Or Not To Be!"
That was the question that I used to utter,
now I slap myself when I start to suffer
the slings and arrows of fortunes outrageous.
I'ma drop rhymes on all the world's stages.
Greatest of the Shakespeare Tragedies--
I'm all H to the A-M-L-E-T.

This is my story, like you've forgotten:
Straight Outta Copenhagen where something was rotten.
A "Prince Of The Realm", I was depress-ed;
My moms remarried, my daddy only two months dead!
Horatio! Yo, he's got my back-
says "Hamlet, I got news and it's kinda whack.
me and the boys were on watch last night,
we saw your daddy's ghost a-walking in the moonlight!"
(Was this Airs from Heaven? Blast from Hell?
Goblin Damned? Spirit Of Health?
You know I had to go see this shit for myself.)
The very next night my DaddyGhost walked,
I pleaded with his shade 'til he finally talked,
"Hamlet, avenge me! And so you know?
Your Uncle is a murderer, yo momma is a ho!"

'Now time is out of joint. Oh cursed spite!
That ever I was born to make it right.'

Then, oh no! Better grab a box of tissues!
Here comes Ophelia with all her issues.
"I love you Hamlet!" Are you makin' fun of me?
Don't go there, girl! Get thee to a nunnery!
(It ain't like I wouldn't want a taste of that,
but the girl's gotta know where a playa's head is at!)
Everyone thinks that I'm crazycrazy!
And all I could think was maybe, I should
just give up? Naw, I ain't drink from that cup...
I'd rather fuck shit up!
A play-within-a-play is just the thing
where I'ma punk the conscience of my Uncle, the King,
and the way he freaked you could easily tell,
that muthafukka was guilty as hell!

My momma told me I was dangerous-mad!
I'm all screaming in her face for betraying my dad.
Then I stabbed Polonius right through the curtain,
that's what the mutthafukka gets for lurking!
I wanted my vengence, so I needed a plan.
Then my uncle sent me off to be murdered in England.
Yo, you roll on me? You're gonna get your ass burned!
...just ask Rosencrantz and Guildenstern.

The Uncle thought he taught me a terminal lesson,
but now I'm back for another session.
To be the Prince Of Denmark, you gotta roll hard,
not just whine like a mopey muthafukka in the graveyard.
Alas, poor Yorick. I knew that bitch,
he was all about the jest, he was infinite.
But now he's dead, 'cause that's the way it goes,
and his skull is just a prop in a stage-show. Yo!
I knew him, Horatio!

Then in rolls a funeral, mourners in tow.
"Who was the corpse?" I wanted to know.
When I saw it was Ophelia I started to shiver.

What made her do a "Jeff Buckley" into the river?
Laertes tried to get all up in my face.
I said "Boy, pick another time, some other place,
and I'll be more than happy to serve you some!
A thousand brother's love couldn't equal my sum!"

My Uncle calls a sword-fight to settle a bet
between me and Laertes. Does he think I'm stupid?
Like I don't see that this is going to be a trap?
Ain't no way that I'm going out like that!

(So now, in the tragedy, we come to Act Five-
you know someone's gonna die...)

My Uncle toasts me, and slips something in the wine,
but my mother drinks first and so then she dies.
Laertes stabs me from behind- a cowardly act
so I take his poisoned sword away and stab his ass back.
Before he dies he wanna do the right thing,
says, "Hamlet, this was all set up by the King!"
So I stabbed him too, forced open his lips,
poured the poison in 'til he choked on it;
held him tight 'til he swallowed it all
and said "Here's a toast to Hell, have a nice fall!"

When the play is over, you can tell this is Shakespeare;
look around the stage, there's dead bodies everywhere.
Yorik says to me "Goodnight Sweet Prince."
But I say "Fuck it- all the rest is silence."

Series Letter #16
by Alveraz Ricardez

Dear Helen,

There is a little native boy outside my hut window. If I move more than two fingers around this pencil he will hear me and alert the tribesman. Last night I was able to bribe him with a piece of carob left over from the care package you sent. He allowed me to pace my room.

Tonight his smile faded when I had *no mas*. Now his marble eyes survey the walls outside, and I'm scared. He reminds me of our son. He has your spindly body, Helen. His caramel skin ashes like yours in the heat. I never understood how your body dried like a *saladito*. Remember when I begged you to sweat? Anyway, he reminds me of Douglas.

When I woke this morning my gut burned. I think it may be malaria, but I'm not sure. It comes in waves now. It must be ten degrees in here. I can see my breath over the words but this parchment is soaked in salt, so I know my body is broken.

Tell Douglas to paint me a picture and hang it over my workbench. Be sure he uses the entire canvas, you now how the white space drives me mad.

I can hear his eyes, Helen, the little native boy. I can hear him sniff at my movements. He has a broken foot, a fishing accident. He drags it when he walks, so I hear him shuffle, drag, shuffle, drag, all around the god damn perimeter.

I think about killing him sometimes. One of my hands could fit around his entire neck, Helen. I could be swift about it. Maybe when this full moon breaks and these crickets realize there is no audience for their orchestra. I don't know. It was just a thought.

I will write again in the morning.

William

...means nothing

by Harris Shumway

...seconds to nothing
minutes to nowhere
change all your clothing
cut off your hair
go with the feeling
piss with the flow
what am i seeing
there's nothing to show...

...chew on the virus
and eat the disease
rape away innocence
and kill the esteem
hit me inside
when you hit her again
your alcohol secrets
are your only friends...

..at all...

...*"father"* means nothing
nothing at all
at all.

Erotic Thoughts Of you

by Jenni Kalicharan

I've been thinking all day of nothing else but you,
Thinking of the love that is shared between us two.
Dreaming of the moments we will be together tonight,
Sharing a passion that can be nothing but right.

Come walk with me now alone on the beach,
I need you tonight, just within my reach.
My body yearns for your gentle touch,
My lips want to please you so very much.

I can't wait to feel your hands in mine,
To imagine your lips on my own, so divine.
I'd love it if you took your tongue for a walk
Cause you won't need it tonight to talk.

Let's make love under the pale moonlight,
Then relax in each other's arms under stars so bright.
Show me just what I mean to you, my sweet,
And I will do the same when on this beach we meet.

CAPE CANAVERAL PORNO

by Bruce Deitrick Price

Blast-off, lift-off, shoot-off...
with spasms of affection,
its X-rated direction
is the sky's slinky grace
and the black hole of space.

A machine obscene and proud
slow-pokes through phosphorescent cloud;
this dick on fire
with hi-tech desire
shames our eyes
and pricks heaven's thighs.

When it has flown
past air and ozone,
my heart sinks.
The sky knows better
and *winks*.

Was it lust or
industrial hum,
white smoke or
transcendental come?

I only know
this is so:
the sexiest sight I ever saw
was this hard-on for a star.

Poem for Mazique

by Caitlin Meissner

Janice says your name three times over,
rolls it around in her mouth.
1, 2...
and I am thinking of your tongue,
but not talking.

It reminds her of magic
mystique
Africa, Mozambique
her unborn grandson.
Janice reminds me that words are important.
You remind me that sometimes they aren't at all.

I talk too fast by nature
and my words spill over
splash on the floor,
messy.
You've taught me the real meaning of
nighttime:
skipping stones
the gentle ripples proving
even rocks can have the illusion
of weightlessness.

Sometimes I whisper that I am
learning to do this all over again
and you say, me too.

Your smells find me at
most inappropriate times.
Sweet smoke through your teeth
coconut oil

and the sweat of desire.
I find my stomach in my throat
somewhere between Jay St
and Herald Square on the F train.

And just sometimes
in the still of midday, midweek
when your face is obscured by covers,
full of sleep
I hear Brooklyn seep through your window
and I wonder.

This is where I quiet my brain
for the world need not be anything more
than this very moment.

The Geography of your History

by John Powers

I feel better knowing She runs along the safe roads
of the rich sections of the city. Lined with grass
bordered sidewalks and huge future houses to be broken
up into tenements once all the rich move to nursing
homes and condos in Florida.

The cars stop at the crosswalks,
let her and the running stroller jog by.

Sometimes, it's easier to recognize the geography of your history
when you wake up thirsty on a plane and see the Appalachians outside
your window seat in miles high textured vapor clouds, and you refuse
the flight attendant's advances (of free water) because you are hoping
as the plane shudders and bounces if the wings fall off and it spits
you out you'll still be thirsty to savor those mountaintops and quench
yourself on the hills and valleys as you fall.

Sometimes, it's easier to keep throwing away water
sealed forever in plastic because its grown too warm sitting
in the car.

- OR -

You spend a few minutes on Sunday calculating spilt milk.
The half ounces left over in each of your son's baby bottles
totaling $264 over a year's time.

None of it is enough to keep you awake unless you let yourself
be amazed at how fast the wind is blowing as your sky becomes
ground.

Momma said There will be days like this...

by Kay Barcelon

My day started with a broken nail
I went to work with a slightly sore finger
Turned a door knob and the door didn't open
Smacked my nose right on the glass pane
I just laughed and went on with my day

With a sore finger and a sore red nose
I checked in for a routine mammogram
The first one was not good I had to do it again
Tech said this time try posing like Cleopatra
Hah! I told her she enjoys inflicting pain

Walking to my car now with a sore chest
I saw an older woman on a wheelchair
Stopped to see if she may need help
Instead with a snarled face she says
What are you looking at and so I left!

Went home with a sore finger, a sore nose
A sore chest and a sore pride
I fixed me a nice plate of Spanish rice
It got too hot my stomach ached
I thought to myself I better quit and go to bed!

Momma said There'll be days like this

You Are DOOMED!!!
Face it, technology has turned you into a wuss
By Victor D. Infante

I've got two new rejection letters on my desk: Poetry Magazine and Fantasy & Science Fiction. Neither rejection can be considered a dishonor, really –while I know folks who've appeared in both of them, they're both notoriously hard to get into, and frankly, while Poetry particularly claims to read everything, they must be amazingly careful handling the paper, because the manuscripts in both cases came back with the paper crisp, the folds undisturbed.

I don't know about anybody else, but I have an immense amount of trouble reading four pieces of paper and then stuffing them into an envelope so neatly as to make them seem undisturbed. Seriously, if they are reading these things, they have levels of care and manual dexterity I am personally unfamiliar with. These folks missed their callings as neurosurgeons.

These aren't the only folks I've got poems and short stories out at right now. Indeed, the A-List literary markets are practically being flooded with my writing. McSweeney's, The Paris Review, The New Yorker, The American Poetry Review – I've quite probably wasted several dollars in postage in recent weeks on the literary equivalent of cleaning the Augean stables in a single day.

Oh, but this little endeavor isn't really about getting published, is it? No, if that were the case, I'd be throwing my work at slightly more reasonable markets, ones where, y'know, cold submissions have a chance in Hell. And the slightly lower tier of lit journals and the like have done well by me in the past. A little elbow grease, and a few of these poems and stories could happily enough be in their pages again, and probably will be once I'm done with this little experiment, although I'll feel a little guilty giving them Poetry's sloppy seconds.

No, upon self-reflection, meditation and drowning out aggression by playing my old Clash albums very loudly, I think I can admit to myself that this whole doomed endeavor is about making sure the boundaries I thought were there really are.

You see, I dislike the idea that I'm doomed. Dislike it immensely. I mean, it's not like any of these publications are publishing material that's, to a page, significantly better than what I've sent them, although some of it definitely is. No, most of it's pretty much the same old crap, particularly the poetry: the sparse, brittle linear narrative leading to the small, quiet personal epiphany. You can hum most of these poems to the same tune, the lyrical structure is so similar: So why the Hell do I care?

I suppose, if I'm honest with myself, there's still a part of my brain that wants the ephemeral prestige and pride that comes with getting something into these publications, the feeling of accomplishment. It's bullshit and psychic debris, but there it is.

Because frankly, I think writers have it too easy these days. Used to be, even just over a decade ago, that putting out a poetry chapbook was hard. Back when I first started out, not everyone had personal computers at home, and even fewer people had whatever Adobe software it is that lets you knock out a chapbook in minutes, particularly if you don't care that the cover sucks. (And judging by most of them these days, most poets really don't.)

Back in the day, these things were mostly done by disreputable types with drinking problems. My first chapbook, put out many, many years ago, was done by a burly punk rocker with a Bukowski fixation, who could write like a thunderstorm but evidently didn't have the typing skills to match. It wasn't just that there were a few typos in the book, it's that it was pretty much all typos, with a few correct words thrown in, and he managed to cut his finger in the process of trimming the pages, so a good stack of the books had blood stains. (This actually happened to me again, with a later chapbook.)

Let's call it an experiment in Dadaism, and be done with it, shall we?

And then there's the Web. I hate to say it, but posting a poem on MySpace isn't the same as getting it published, and I'm afraid I have to raise my eyebrows at anyone who thinks it is. (And I run across them. Regularly. I find it depressing.) Now, if your goal is to share your work with your friends and family, that's fine, but really, don't try to convince me it's an equivalent experience as getting it published somewhere where there's actually a selection process. It's not a bad thing, but it's not an accomplishment, either.

I'm all for DIY, but let's face it, it's gotten way too easy to do it yourself. Just because your fate's in your own hands and not in the hands of some indifferent editor with an ugly shirt and a mild sexual dysfunction doesn't mean you get to slack off.

The sad truth is, if you're letting Microsoft and Kinko's do all the actual work for you, then it's really not much of an accomplishment, is it? If you're going to go this route, find some way to make the chapbook something unique, something different than all the processed cheese out there. If it's not actual work, you're doing it wrong.

I'm not saying you need to bleed for your art, I'm just saying that if you aren't bleeding for your art, you're a wimp. And that's a perfectly valid lifestyle choice.

paper dragons

by Mary Ward

we are paper dragons
dancing through the streets
choked with crowds.
two hearts
oceans apart.

your eyes, fire crackers,
surprising my soul.
how deep your gaze.

my offerings,
sweet,
mere candy
for your hungry mouth.

I try to speak a flood of words
but they drown
under this canopy of color,
whiskers, wings and scales.

with hidden arms
we cannot touch.

a flame could set us afire.

we dance for one another
fragile, frenzied.

and you pray for rain.

If Only You Knew

by Melanie Reid

Maybe one day
Ill get another taste
You left my mouth watering for more
man
I do adore the things you do to me

When we were one
you touched every inch of me
passion was real
now I cant even deal

While having sex with another
I cant help but to picture
you standing in front
butt a*s hole nude
girl
dude had the biggest thing
you would think it hurt
no no no
you just don't know
chills up my spine
that was the best sin-sation ever
and I do mean sin

If only you knew

For Emily

By Jonathan Chin

After James Merrill

The river's only where Manhattan stops
encroaching on the sky. You chose this place
for its solemnity. You try to place
her ersatz look among the crowded tops

of heads emerging from the Hudson stairs.
You worry that too much has changed these past
two years to notice if she had walked past
but she appears, smiling and unaware

that she is late. You take seats in the shade by the grass
still fenced in February. She asks about
your writing, her tone of voice you'd forgot about
till now. You extract from a bag a bundled mass

of papers. She flips through them while mouthing out
the syncopations that she taught you how
to write. This while she bobs her head to how
your iambs enjamb. You watch her there without

a word, that other lesson that took you
this long to learn. She says she has to leave,
you stand only the receive the ruffled leaves
of a chapbook instead of a kiss; that must do

for goodbye. You wonder how she remains
unchanged by the world. Those days you loved her were for
her naivety. Even now she waits for
a smile before she goes; a smile you feign.

What would happen if you delayed? Chance encounter
in Boston, cities apart, a loss of words
would rob you of the split second for words
you have for "I'm sorry." Instead this flattened river

and its look of oblivion calms your nerves.

Cabbages/

by K. Eltinaé

I remember the moment when I knew for sure,
I sat gawking at your knees,
Jutting like fists,
Twin cabbages,
Two stubborn minds made up,
You were counting numbers,
Until my tongue slipped into a sea,
Of all the things you'd done for me,
The blame washed in and settled
I had used my last chance,
And your words could no longer save me.

I remember your quivering knees,
Like the knobs of two doors,
I listened to your moist hands,
Breathe and sweat,
Sans regret.

You have two hearts,
Who have never come to terms with each other.
They are wrapped in inches and inches of cabbage skin,
They are dangerously polar.
You've kept them apart
Auctioning each discretely,
But I am secretly afraid for you,
I hear them snap and lock,
Snarling, like the kept prisoners they are,
Your smile is growing less and less convincing
Nothing will save you from the floor.

I stare closely at your knees,
Willing their chambers free,

Once your last words descend,
I hear each of your hearts explode.
Your expression is a picture,
Collapsing like a yielding tent,
The floor beckons to you.

"the neil diamond poem": my poem about jeans (for sam)

By Natey Hutnak

(or, my poem about jeans for sam)

i remember once
i met, or, rather,
there was this girl
that met me.
she wore the tightest
faded in all the right
places jeans i ever seen
on a woman, before sam...
and her name was
like a song
on the tip of
your tongue
forgotten, until you
hear it again
and for a
split second
you flip through your
mind, and then-
oh my god its!
neil diamond.
and you realize that
for the last
twelve hours
you have been having a
neildiamondexperience
in your head!
you went around
humming everywhere
all day

asking people
if they knew what it was
everyone was SO supportive
but no connections
it
started out
like around nine am
and some people said
it was a pink
floyd tune and
you were sure it was
some psycho dellic tune
then noon came and
some people said it was
the theme song to mickie dees
all beef patties special
sauce lettuce cheese
pickles onions on a
sesame seed bun....
by three pm you were
totally convinced it was
whoop there it is
and you kept picturing
women running
around in those
tight daisy duke
jean shorts and
tacky red blouses all
tied in a knot
so that you could
see all the bellybuttons
and the women were all
beautiful cowgirls with long
hair and smiles with big white
tits, i mean, teeth!
teeth!
there weren't singing or

nothin
just sort of
posing like penthouse playmates
or somethin
and smilin like
they were smiling
RIGHT AT YOU
and no one else
not even the guy behind
the guy operating the
video equipment but
RIGHT AT YOU
and all your adolescent friends
sitting next to you on your moms
couch, the same couch
that your dog likes to
sneak naps on every once in a while
(cuz you let him, of course)
and that makes fleas...
cause he always plays in the dirt
behind your house and
WHOOP THERE IT IS!
there WHAT is?
what the fuck does
whoop
mean anyway?!
whoop there it is!
i don't know.
but i do know this.
around like, nine pm
this guy starts
hummin the same song
you are hummin
and your hummin
and he is hummin
and now your both
hummin this song

and he looks at
you and says "hey"
(like you have
fruit flies the size
of kellog's frosted
mini wheats
circling around your head)
"hey, aren't you a bit
young to be hummin
neil diamond songs?"
so you say "as a
matter of fact...
what is the name of
this song?"
and he says "i thank
the lord for the nighttime."
so you start telling
him how that song is
like this girl's name...

remember the girl?
you know, the girl
she wore the tightest
faded in all the right
places jeans i ever seen
and she spoke
like no other woman could
i met her only twice.
tonight
and then one year earlier
i forgot her name
remembered the jeans
yeah forgot her name
because her name was
like a song
on the tip of
your tongue

forgotten, until you
hear it again
and for a
split second
you flip through your
mind, and
wonder if anyone
realizes that you are
actually reading the
same poem over
and over again
and might actually
get away with it
if it weren't for the
fact that at least one
person in the room
is actually listening
to you and not just
watching you and falling
asleep with their eyes
open
because you have been
up here at least
3 minutes now
babbling about
naked bellybuttons
or some fool thing
and half of the people awake
are waiting for the
mickie dees jingle
to come around again.
but it won't!
cause it's not
dinner time
and you don't want to
fuck with people
in these circumstances

because they might just
eat you... oh, yeah
you wish!
great, now they think
you're a chauvanist
pig
just because
you are a bit more
open and honest
than some other
assholes
who ever so subtly
tell you they wanna
sleep with you
and ever so covertly
tell you how
beautiful you would
look riding their
clydesdales
and of course
you eat it all up!
because you
just like me
are starving for
love and attention
and affection
and a feeling of
comfort
and you just like me
want more intimacy
and less
banshi sex
in your life
because you
are sick of the thought
of lying in your deathbed
at thirty...something

dying of some
unknown disease
that you can't remember
who
or
when
or
where
or
why
or how many people
it infected
because you were just
stupid at one time
(or several)
or another...
you don't want that!
YOU DON'T WANT THAT!

so you forget a name
just means you got more
on your mind already to
remember

you forget the name
but at least
you get the
jeans part right.

The Night Anna Got Religion
By CA Jackson

there were crickets
i remember that
and just the faint
sound of
Lodi
on the radio
the only lights were
reflecting from
her eyes
and i swear
that was an
awakening,
momentary,
from this dream of flesh.
it started cold
eventually ending
up sweaty
she had
to slam her
hand over her mouth
at the sheer
immensity of
the volume of
heaven,
i just closed
my eyes
and pushed through
the great cloud
of
her Tathagata.
resting on
our cloud
the radio finally switched

over to
Love You To.

I had sex with my mother-in-law

by Randy Johnson

(This is a fictional poem)

When she turned on the lights, I screamed and screamed.
I pinched myself because I was hoping it was all just a dream.
It was the most horrible thing I ever saw.
I had sex with my mother-in-law.
She was in the bed that my wife and I slept in.
Now I'm so turned off by sex that I may never get horny again.
While touching her breasts, I thought it was odd because they were wrinkled and seemed to sag.
I nearly died of heart failure when I saw who I shagged.
I can't get the vision of that gray hair, wrinkled skin, and false teeth out of my mind.
But what bothers me the most is that I squeezed that prune shaped behind.
My wife started insisting that the three of us have a menage a trois.
I said not with my mother-in-law.
My wife said she'd leave me if I didn't stop saying no.
I pointed toward the door and I said go.

Bright White Polar Bears

by Michael Jeffreys

Step across the top of stars
and look down around the moon
dream along a coast of blue
or wade in a gold lagoon

Wish into a blade of grass
or touch a fallen tear
hold a smile from someone's face
and turn away the fear

Think of bright white polar bears
and frosty crystal snow
or bluish clouds of summer rain
and feel the four winds blow

Walk into the daylight
under rainbows far and near
or leave a little something kind
for loved ones that are dear

Haight Love

by Michael Firewalker

[remembering Haight-Ashbury, 1974]

A rocker sways
In kaftan grays
Patchouli lays
Its spicey haze
Dylan screams
His gravel tunes
Needles burn to
Hot tattoos
Lonely strings
Play moody blues
For flower children
Learning who's
The newest craze
In righting wrongs
With protest songs
Mellow Yellow
Vietnam
Dying fellows
Killing Cong
Rainbow lovers
Kissing sisters
Saffron brothers
Marching blisters
Midnight strokes
In heavy musk
Smoking tokes
With angel dust
Silken scarves
Hide roping scars
On Jesus Christ

Superstar
Forgotten women
Unrepentant
Unforgiven
Paint their faces
Shoot up fate
Hang their laces
Filled with flowers
Fragrant graces
Power hours
Lovin' freedom
In the Haight

As they retreated.

By zan

They lit the olive trees

Whole orchards burned

Two-three hundred-year-old woods
Fizzing and popping
In the night
Moaning and groaning
About being alight
The beauty of the flames
Hiding the tragedy

I put the rifle
To my ear
I can hear the sea
The waves crashing
In my mind
Too far away
To put out the pyre

A devils island
The orchard burns
An oasis of death
Yet life abundant
As embers fly
Like evil nymphs.

The houses smolder
But with less innocence

More deserving
They fall to their knees

They! die quickly.

My palestinian Girl (For a very special lady)
by Karim M. Sewilam

My palestinian girl,
You make the world appear pale,
Because you shine in radiant grace,
That nature cannot imitate.

My palestinian girl,
when i look into your eyes
I see parallel universes of magic and elegancy
that no one imagined to exist.

My palestinian girl,
Moon light envies you,
because as magical as it is,
It cannot move the hearts of humans as you do.

My palestinian girl,
It seems that when your tiny feet treads the ground,
Earth sings a joyfull song
That only i can hear.

My palestinian girl
War scars the human soul,
But yours, still pure still crystal clear
That i can see through it magical forms and endless stars.

My palestinian girl,
Hold your head up high
Because you are the spirit of your nation,
And the beat of my heart.

My palestinian girl,
When i touch your hand

And our souls meet, a heavenly glow
Is seen through the spectrums of eternity.

My palestinian girl,
When you smile ,
Creatures of the wild learn that peace
Is possible through love.

My palestinian girl,
Shine on, and know that,
Your beauty is the secret language of eternity
and i am one of the a few that learned it.

My palestinian girl,
We live by the sea,
Lost in our passion,
Listening to the whispers that nature to us speak.

My palestinian girl,
You will always be
The angel that captivates
My Mind ,heart and soul.

(samar ,your love runs in my veins)

About the Poets and Authors

Deb Powers
chameleon
Worcester, MA
Just a middle-aged lady creeping on toward senior status and wondering when the hell she stopped being 18

Liv
No real name
No Biography

Megan Andelman
redheadedslxt
North Dighton, MA
Writing has been the most rewarding addiction... Veering away from the road traveled by the masses takes us to places we could never have imagined. I met my fiancé on GotPoetry; since then my life has become filled with unexpected twists and amazing surprises.

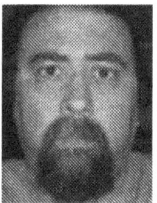
Tony Brown
Tony
Worcester, MA
Tony Brown, 47, has been writing poetry for over thirty years and is one of the administrators of Gotpoetry.com.

Susan Voth
hotstuff
Moncton, NB Canada
Susan was born in Edmonton, AB on April 11th and has lived most of her life in Moncton, NB. Currently

residing in Fredericton, she has just published her first book of poetry entitled Liquored Words & Afterthoughts. Visit her site at www.susanvoth.com

J. Bradley
nerdthuggery
Orlando, FL

j. bradley is a refugee from the planet Cybertron. He transforms into an 8-year-old boy who can shoot Nerd darts from his fingers. His work has been featured in edifice Wrecked, Orlando Sentinel, and Look Up At The Sky: Poems About Comic Books

Cody J. Czerniak
No used Id given
No Biography

Ben Alan Brownlow
BenBrownlow
Monitor, WA

Ben Brownlow came out alright on the ass end of an existential crisis and now resides in a double wide on an orchard where he enjoys composting, playing pool on crooked tables, commuting unhealthy distances on recycled bicycles, and making love until sunrise.

Paul David Mena
Haikupoet
Boston and environs

Paul is a poet, technologist, cynic, father of five, child of chaos, punker, prankster, patriot, punster, leftist, latino, japanophile, audiophile, beer drinker, quiche eater, dog walker, soft talker, deep thinker, shallow sleeper, introvert, covert operative in a parallel universe.

DIMITRIUS
New York
No Biography

Mick Scott
mick4himself
Montgomery. Alabama
Osmosis.Poet is the stage name of Mitchell "Mick" Scott, who is very talented poet and speaks about the balances of life from religion to real world issues, and more. He began writing poetry in the form of rap music at the age of fifteen.

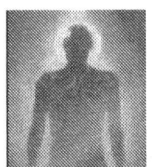
Bill Burgos
brownbwi
Los Angeles
My name is Bill Burgos. I am a thirty four year old illustrator, designer raised in los angeles california. I gained an appreciation for poetry in the early 90"s after moving to brooklyn, new york.

Afrika Midnight Asha Abney
Afrika
Washington, DC
Afrika Midnight Asha Abney is a Native Washingtonian, freelance poet, freelance writer, former host and events coordinator, and author. For more information please visit http://www.authorsden.com/afrikamaabney and http://www.clearblogs.com/afrikamaabney

Bret Wooldridge
Arpeggio
Boulder Creek, CA
Bret is a rock and jazz guitarist with a weakness for Mexican food and oriental poetry. He works in the traffic control business. Cars not planes.

Joe Fusco Jr.
bardofaisle9
Worcester, MA
Joe Fusco, Jr. has been the featured poet at venues all over Massachusetts, including Java Hut, Moonstruck Café, Plantation Club and Poet's Parlor. Among his chapbooks are the titles Death and Other Happy Endings, and Poems I Don't Read at Barnes & Noble. His poems have appeared in Worcester Magazine, Ominvore, Lancaster Times and elsewhere. Joe has been in the supermarket business for twenty-eight years; he lives in Worcester. Joe has written eighteen songs, likes to read serial-killer novels and plays in a forty-and-over basketball league. He loves to eat!

Ryk McIntyre
rykmcintyre
Providence, RI
Ryk McIntyre has reinvented himself more times than he cares to admit. A Boston slam poet since 1991, Ryk's work is ranges from humorous to heavy, from slam to the page and back again. He is a regular columnist here at GotPoetry.com. Check out his Bilbio - Other Bible Stories column. Bilbio is a series of short stories, thematically linked, that retell Bible stories from different perspectives. They are written by Ryk McIntyre and published serially every month.

Alveraz Ricardez
Hot_Mud
Los Angeles, CA
Alveraz Ricardez is the editor of Kill Poet Press & Journal. He has been published in Chronogram, Voodoo Beat, MiPoesias, Pemmican, Softblow, and numerous other journals. He is traveling on a national book tour in January in support of his volume of poetry, Hot Mud Poems. His second volume, The Pill Bug Torero will be published in February. He works as a screenwriter in Hollywood and lives with his wife and two children.

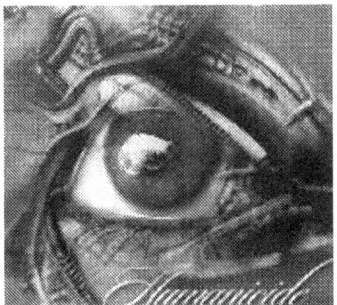
Harris Shumway
Humanicide
North Dighton, MA
"You can't resist her / She's in your bones / She is your marrow / And your ride home / You can't avoid her / She's in the air (in the air) / In between molecules / Of oxygen and carbon dioxide..." –rivers coumo

Jenni Kalicharan
Islandgrrl
Trinidad & Tobago
I have been married to the love of my life for the past 28 years. I am the Principal of a small primary school. I have no children but I have been blessed in raising my little sister and her son. I have two poetry books published.

Bruce Deitrick Price
brucedeitrickprice
Norfolk, VA
Author of four books (novels and nonfiction)....Have written poetry all my life....Write about education and culture, etc. for my site Improve-Education.org.... Did so much digital art with the left, I've had to become right-handed with the mouse.

Caitlin Meissner
caitlin.meissner
Brooklyn, New York
With a combination of words, heart-Braille and painful life lessons, performance poet Caitlin Meissner uses her activist background in anti-racism work, disability advocacy and youth empowerment as a platform on the human experience.

John Powers
John
Providence, RI
John Powers is a national performing poet out of Rhode Island. No it's not an actual island. It's the smallest state in the union. He was born in December of 1971 in London England. At an early age he immigrated to the United States but maintains dual citizenship. He lost his accent long ago.

Kay Barcelon
KayBarcelon
Philippines
Smile and be pleasant... A good way to start the day !!

Victor D. Infante
Ocvictor
Worcester, MA
Victor D. Infante has, in no particular order, been worshiped as a god by a subterranean race of mole men, battled Nazi Spies on the edge of Hoover Damn, and single-handedly reunited the small town of Truth or Consequences, New Mexico, after the brief but unsettling incident involving Mrs. O'Leary's prize-winning quiche, of which no more will be spoken.

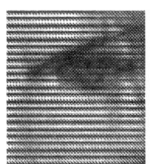
Mary Ward
mayo
Cambridge, MA
Surrounded by children or arguing over beer in a Harvard Square pub, star gazing, tending a garden or milking a goat, I always carry enough Hope to smile. And I sometimes write poetry to hear some soul sing.

Melanie Reid
No username
No Biography given

Jonathan Chin
jonathanchin
NYC / Boston
Jonathan Chin is a computer savant turned performance poet. He left behind the unsung glory of computer programming for the self sung grandeur of slam. Originally from New York City, he is currently a student at Boston University but not for long...

K. Eltinaé
k.eltinaé
Sudan
K. Eltinaé is a poet from the Sudan, who has been

writing from a young age. "Cabbages" is taken from his forthcoming anthology "Chagrin".

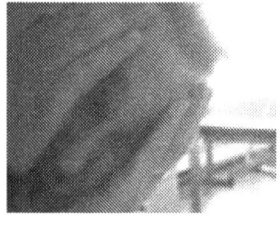

Natey Hutnak
Natey
Providence, RI
Nathan Hutnak walked around random places in New England for a couple years collecting poems on scraps of paper and napkins from random poets. He sold the site to John Powers for gas money in 2001. John does a good job. It's better than CATS.

CA Jackson
unknownothers
Norman, OK
Born in 1986 in Lubbock, Texas, I spent most of my life in the Pacific Northwest. I began writing at age 18 on a whim and have been at it since. Most of my time is spent between work, writing and worship.

Randy Johnson
randy-johnson
Tennessee
I was born August 20, 1971. I've lived in Tennessee since 1973. I've been writing since 1980. I dropped out of school in 1986 at the age of fifteen but I later graduated high school in 1995. I am also a BMI songwriter.
My first poem was published in 1996.

Michael Jeffreys
Michael
Mojave Desert, California
Husband, Father of two, designer of furniture and related cabinetry, pursuing poetry and writing, and big fan of gotpoetry.

MichaelFirewalker
No real name
Seattle
a butch who loves Light, Mother Earth, human sexuality, nearly all forms of spirituality, but has no respect whatsoever for religion...

zan
No real name
No Biography

Karim M. Sewilam
MadPoet
Cairo, Egypt
visit my website WWW.BLACK-SHEEP-SOCIETY.COM

www.ingramcontent.com/pod-product-compliance
Lightning Source LLC
Chambersburg PA
CBHW021022090426
42738CB00007B/872